Imagined Realities

Previous Books:

Imagined Realities

by

Arthur O.R. Thormann

Specfab Industries Ltd.

Edmonton, Alberta

2019

Thormann, Arthur O. R. (Arthur Otto Rudolf), 1934-, author
    Imagined Realities

ISBN 978-0-9916849-9-1

Publisher: Specfab Industries Ltd.
                        13559 - 123A Avenue
                        Edmonton, Alberta, Canada
                        T5L 2Z1
                        Telephone: 780-454-6396

Publication assistance by

PAGEMASTER
PUBLISHING
PageMaster.ca

Cover Designs: Front: Question Mark depicts Reality
                        Back: Text by author; image citation:
                        Weisstein, Eric W. "Young Girl-Old Woman
                        Illusion." From Mathworld—a Wolfram Web
                        Resource. http://mathworld.wolfram.com

The true sign of intelligence
is not knowledge
but imagination.
Albert Einstein

I dedicate this book to those who use their imagination!

My gratitude also goes to my daughters Nancy & Diana for their valued edits. All mistakes remaining are mine.

Author's Note

I started this book as my third attempt to write *Conclusions Volume III.* However, the further I got into it, the more I realized that a better title for the book would be *Imagined Realities,* but I also still intend to write the third volume of *Conclusions*, and so be patient.

This book is about imagination, thus the question mark on the front cover. I'll leave the young girl on the back cover to your imagination.

Arthur O.R. Thormann
May 2019

Contents

Imagined Realities

People will imagine all sorts of things, which they will try to connect to realities. They'll imagine their creation and the one who might have created them, and even the one who might have created their creator. They'll imagine what their afterlife might be like, even when there might not be an afterlife. They'll imagine how their lives might end, and so on. Imagined realities are, after all, more enjoyable than realities often are. Sometimes, people will even try to imagine the unimaginable, such as zero and infinity.

A friend of mine sent me a book by Roger Penrose called The Road to Reality. The friend wanted me to read what Roger Penrose had to say about zero. However, what interested me more was the title of the book: if we were on the road to reality, where, in fact, were we? As Penrose says in the final chapter:

"I hope it is clear, from the discussion given in the previous sections, that our road to understanding the nature of the real world is still a long way from its goal. Perhaps this goal will never be reached, or perhaps there will eventually emerge some ultimate theory, in terms of which what we call 'reality' can in principle be understood. If so, the nature of that theory must differ enormously from what we have seen in physical theories so far."

In other words, Penrose is saying we do not understand reality, and perhaps never will understand it, unless some theory comes up to help us understand it. So, are we, perhaps, being still stuck in a sphere of unreality, and traveling on the road to reality? Of course, Penrose's reality consists of a mathematical reality, which is quite foreign to the rest of us mortals. By the way, Penrose did not say much about zero.

I want to mention two aspects for you to think about: The first is an unimaginable, like zero! If you try to think of nothing at all, you'll find it impossible!

The second aspect is either nonexistent or unknowable; however, you can create an imaginable reality for this aspect; for example, for God you can create a kindly old man with a white beard; for heaven, you can create a calm and sunny countryside; for the devil, you can create a fierce creature with horns and a tail; for angels, you can create young girls in white robes with wings on their backs; and so on. Thus, the unknowable, which may also be nonexistent, can be given an imaginable reality, without ever having a known reality!

*

This book is about imagined realities. The reality is

that most realities are preceded by imagined realities: whether imagining winning a bet in a casino; whether imagining being protected by fail-safe measures; whether imagining being resigned to things that happen; whether imagining that risks in business affect only others; whether imagining that life goes on forever; whether imagining that the future will be better or worse than the past; and so on; all these imagined realities hope for some reality.

Wherever possible, I tried to give illustrations of my own imagined realities. For example, when I listened to my Sunday school teacher describing heaven, and how we would end up there if we lived a life without sin, this led to an imagined reality that I could actually end up in such a wonderful place, although I realized later in life that this imagined reality may, in fact, never become a reality. This could also be so with many other imagined realities, such as the hope of being reincarnated.

Nevertheless, imagined realities that eventually end up in realities are very useful to the development and progress of the human race – to wit, all the imagined inventions.

Imagined realities often support feelings of hope. When a person is in hospital with a serious illness, it is his or her imagined reality that creates a future of wellness, or it is his or her assurance of friends that all will be fine. Also, when a person goes on a vacation, hoping to visit a country with a warmer climate, his or her imagined reality supports that hope. It can be a healthful imagined reality, even if it never leads to a reality.

The reality is that an imagined reality precedes a reality, if the reality exists at all, but the imagined reality can easily be an illusion, a fantasy, a dream, or a figment of one's imagination. I hope you will enjoy the examples of imagined realities that I provided you in this book, but please remember that not all imagined realities will end up in realities.

Many years ago when I wrote my poems, they were full of imagined realities, and I decided to include some excerpts of them in an appendix of this book. I'll give you an example:

Forlorn I sit upon the beach / and let the waves engulf my feet; / my heart is out there with the maids; / my spirit's singing with a beat. / And soon my being is engulfed / by waters of emotions torn / between realities and dreams, / and soon I feel I'm not yet born.

Well, enjoy your own imagined realities. Perhaps most of them will become pleasant realities.

Creation

The very word "creation" is a mystery. When human beings create a thing, they usually start with something. A painter starts with a canvas and paint to create an image; the singer starts with vocal cords to create a song; the musician starts with an instrument to create music; and so on. However, according to the Bible authors, God started with nothing except His name to create the entire universe.[*]

On the first day, God created the heaven and the earth, and light – presumably from the Sun, but the Sun was not created until the fourth day. On the second day, God created the firmament, which He called heaven. On the third day, God divided the water and created land, grass, herbs, and trees yielding fruit. On the fourth day, God created the Sun, the Moon, and the stars. On the fifth day, God created great whales and fishes and the fowls. On the sixth day, God created the beasts, cattle, creeping things, and man, a male and a female in His own image.[†] However, man was not created from nothing. The male, was created

---

[*] St. John tells us, "In the beginning was the Word, and the Word was with God, and the Word was God."
[†] Genesis 1:1-31

5

from dust, and the female was created from one of the male's ribs.

Let's have a look at the stars that God created from nothing on the fourth day of His creative activity. There are about ten billion galaxies in the visible universe! The number of stars in a galaxy varies, but assuming an average of one hundred billion stars per galaxy means that there are about one billion trillion stars in the visible universe (that's a one with twenty-one zeros)! Along with the stars come their planets, of course. Assuming each star has an average of ten planets, there would also be ten billion trillion planets in the visible universe. Furthermore, along with the planets come their moons, so it is reasonable to assume there would also be ten billion trillion moons in the visible universe! In addition, we have untold numbers of other cosmic bodies in the visible universe, like asteroids, comets, and meteoroids, and if there were only one million of these per star, we can add another one million billion trillion cosmic bodies to the visible universe. You must admit, this is quite an accomplishment for a day's creation!

Of course, our scientists have a different version of our universe's creation, which they attribute to the Big Bang that happened 13.8 billion years ago. At that time, all matter of our universe, including the galaxies, the stars, and the planets, was concentrated in an area no bigger than the point of a pin, and the Big Bang released this matter to form the galaxies, the stars, and the planets as we now know them. Presumably, this pinpoint also contained God, who might even have caused the Big Bang. However, not even the Big Bang was created from nothing – it was all there, before the Big Bang! Had the authors of the Bible known about the Big Bang, they might have written an entirely different theory concerning the creation of our universe.

However, the biggest and greatest creation mystery is the mystery of life. Our scientists are still puzzled by this creation. God might smile and say to them: Listen, you guys, I gave each of you a brilliant mind to solve this mystery. I gave you all the means on Earth to do it, like the physical, chemical, and biological means. So don't go traipsing off to Mars and the rest of the universe to find the answer. You have everything you need right here on Earth. Use the brilliant mind I gave you, as you have done to determine that the Big Bang created the universe. Find another "Big Bang" that created life. Be patient. If time lacks, there is always eternity.* And if you're stymied, read the Bible to find out how I did it: "And the Lord God formed man of the dust of the ground,

---

* This is actually an assertion by Henry Miller from his book *Big Sur and the Oranges of Hieronymus Bosch.*

and breathed into his nostrils the breath of life; and man became a living soul."[*]

But our scientists just shake their heads and say: How do we know what was in God's breath that created life? Was it hot? Was it cool? Was it sweet? Was it foul? How do we know what was in it? We are truly stymied! We can't even create life in a single cell, or in one amoeba, or even in one bacterium.

It makes you wonder, doesn't it? No wonder our "brilliant" scientists cannot conquer diseases like cancer, although they can more easily find the creation of our universe. God, still smiling, might say to them: "You look for me in oddest places and do not recognize my faces, but I am there for you to see, and my secret is…Simplicity!"[†]

So, as you can see, not only is the very word "creation" a mystery, but so is everything it stands for, especially concerning the creation of our universe, and the creation of life itself! However, all is not lost; as long as our scientists, with the brilliant minds God endowed them, keep working at it to find the answers!

---

[*] Genesis 2:7
[†] This is actually an assertion by the author from his poem *The One And All*.

The Afterlife

Christians like heaven for their afterlife, and serious sinners are promised to go to hell. When I was a boy, I had an imaginative Sunday school teacher. He described for us children what a wonderful place heaven was like. The trees and fields were a lush green, never needing water to maintain their color. Flowers were blooming everywhere, all year around. Friendly lions and other friendly beasts were walking in the fields, no longer interested in devouring each other and human beings. Angels were singing softly for the pleasure of humans. God paid a visit each day to bless everyone. The teacher went on and on describing the wonderful things in heaven – every misery on Earth was eliminated and replaced with all the niceties of heaven, and we children became more and more anxious to go there.

Every Sunday, we wanted to know more about this wonderful place called heaven, and the teacher obliged us with further details. Would we get our favorite ice-cream? Yes. Would we get Hawaiian pizza? Yes. Where would God get the ham to make Hawaiian pizza? The teacher gave that some thought, because he did not want to tell us that God would kill pigs. Then he told us, God would order the ham from Earth. Occasionally, the teacher would digress and tell us about the awful place hell. He warned us not to become sinners who would end up there. He said hell was a very hot place and we would surely fry there, and the Devil would come and rub his hands and laugh at us. To stay out of hell, the teacher warned us not to be sinful. Well, the teacher certainly had us children convinced that heaven was a much better place to go to than hell. There is no doubt in my mind that the Sunday school teacher himself was living in an imagined reality, which is not uncommon – many people live there.

Jewish folk are assured that their souls, that is, the spirits that were with them during their lives on Earth, return to God. This assurance comes from the Bible: "By the sweat of your face you shall eat bread until you return to the ground, for out of it you were taken; you are dust, and to dust you shall return," (Genesis 3:19) "and the spirit returns to God who gave it." (Ecclesiastes 12:7) Well, there you have it. That's where the Jewish people's soul goes after the death of the body, back to God – another imaginative reality.

Hinduists, Jainists, Sikhists, and Buddhists, of course, all want to be reincarnated after death. They want to come back to Earth after they die and give life on Earth another try – either as another human being, or even as some beast or a mosquito. Reincarnation is also called rebirth or transmigration, which is part of the Saṃsāra doctrine of cyclic existence. A belief of rebirth was held by Greek figures like Pythagoras, Socrates, and Plato, and is also a common belief of religions like Spiritism, Theosophy, and Eckankar, as well as many tribal societies around the world. A typical reincarnated figure in our times is the 14th Dalai Lama. Skeptic Carl Sagan asked the Dalai Lama what he would do if a fundamental tenet of his religion (reincarnation) were definitively disproved by science. The Dalai Lama answered, "If science can disprove reincarnation, Tibetan Buddhism would abandon reincarnation…, but it's going to be mighty hard to disprove reincarnation." (Wikipedia) Reincarnation is certainly a very imaginative reality – even Salvador Dali believed he was the reincarnation of his dead brother.

Many people, even nonreligious people, believe the soul will continue to live after death of the body. This belief is nothing more than the vanity that makes people want to live forever. These people are so awed by their superior existence that it's hard to believe that their existence will simply cease one day. Thus, they transfer themselves to an imagined reality in order to create the continuance of their Earthly lives.

Robert Lanza M.D., Biocentrism, tells us: "The idea of the soul is bound up with the idea of a future life and our belief in a continued existence after death.

"The commonest mental operations – such as imagination and memory – suggest the existence of a vital life force that exists independent of the body. Yet, the current scientific paradigm doesn't recognize this spiritual dimension of life. Just this year a team of physicists showed that quantum weirdness also occurs in the human-scale world. Importantly, this has a direct bearing on the question of whether humans and other living creatures have souls. The results not only defy our classical intuition, but suggest that a part of the mind – the soul – is immortal and exists outside of space and time."

Here is an afterlife idea I would like to submit to our scientists for assessment: every person has thoughts, and these thoughts might be transmitted into the cosmos by mysterious radio waves, and might eventually be received by another living person – most of us have experienced some form of *déjà vu*. Thus, these thoughts could well become the afterlife of the person who transmitted them. It's a possibility, but it's still in the realm of imagined realities, until its existence can be proven.

Terminus

We learn from early childhood onward that death is inevitable. It is not an easy thing to learn, but it is one of the sadnesses of life that doesn't spare anyone. When I was a boy, I literally grew up with death all around me, and learning that death was inevitable was a little harder for me to grasp because death around me was caused by a terribly raging war – death was evitable. However, when I grew older, and people around me were dying of natural causes, only then the realization that death is actually inevitable became clear to me. Nevertheless, the logic of this was harder to learn, because it was backed up by my elders with assurances like "the only certainties in life are death and taxes."

In 1967, Canada's one-hundred's anniversary, my maternal grandfather was eighty-three years old and suffering from diabetes. His eyesight was failing him, but he still read the New Testament of the Bible every day. His Bible had two columns: the left column had the English translation, and the right column had the German translation. He liked to compare the translations and point out differences to me. However, as he was turning more and more blind, his will to live also disappeared. He never told me that he was afraid to die, but he obviously didn't look forward to a life of blindness. He passed away on Christmas Eve 1967.

Although I missed my grandfather, I considered his death natural and as such it did not affect me much. However, when my good friend Gwyn Davies died of an apparent suicide three months later, it hit me hard. Gwyn was my age, and we had spent much time together. Besides, his death seemed evitable to me, and I mourned over it as I had never mourned before or afterwards.

When my Uncle Alex was hospitalized because of a cancer treatment he had to receive, I paid him a visit. I just looked at him, and he looked at me. He and I were never real close. When I left Germany, I gave him my stamp collection. It was a valuable collection because it contained most if not all of the stamps Germany had issued, and he never told me what he did with it when he came to Canada. He did offer me a job to work on my grandfather's farm, which Uncle Alex intended to take over. We looked at each other for more than a minute, and then he said, "Endstation," the German word for terminus, meaning, he would not recover from his disease. He died shortly after my visit. Terminus – the end of a railway line – well put by Uncle Alex, I thought: the end of one's life, although many people believe that life continues somehow; Uncle Alex evidently did not believe this.

Just before my mother died, I had some conversations with her, and I had the feeling that she was unsure about what would happen to her after death. She was always a religious woman, although floundering a bit in her religions, I thought, but the prospect of death did give her some concerns. This is not uncommon with religious people who are concerned about their sins and whether they'll make it into the next life because of their sins.

My mother's other brothers, Uncle Albert and Uncle Rudi, were also religious people. Uncle Albert ended up with Alzheimer's disease, and when I paid him a visit just before he died, he did not even recognize me, so I doubt if death gave him any concerns. Uncle Rudi was a religious fanatic. I believe he felt extremely righteous, probably with few, if any, sins. I chastised him once when he insisted that I don't bring his estranged wife to one of their daughters' weddings. I thought that Christian people were supposed to love their enemies, and I told him so. When I visited him in his last days in hospital, he gave me a strange look. My earlier criticism of his unloving attitude towards his estranged wife must have still bothered him, although I'm sure his other sinless life gave him the needed comfort to get into heaven.

Since my maternal grandfather died, I lost about fifty friends and relatives. Quite a few of them succumbed to the disease of cancer, a terrible disease that our medical geniuses should have conquered by now. My friend Gordon Hammond was the owner of a Boston Pizza franchise. Naturally, we enjoyed a few pizzas together. One day, I noticed his eyelids were unusually swollen. When I mentioned this, he made light of it and blamed it on some imbalance in his body. But eventually he developed other symptoms, and he told me that he had contracted some sort of cancer. He bought a motor home, and he and Renee, his second wife, went traveling for a while. She fed him profusely with vitamins, in the hope to subdue or kill the cancer, but eventually he was hospitalized. I paid him a few visits at the W.W. Cross Hospital and at one such visit, just as he was receiving chemotherapy, I noticed a huge swelling in his abdomen. He assured me he was feeling fine and would be out of there as soon as he got rid of this thing – pointing to his abdomen. A few days later he died. I believe he had not expected to die. Terminus was not envisioned by him. The imagined reality for many people is to live forever, either on Earth or somewhere in our universe.

Resignation

The philosophical idea of resignation came home to me while reading W. Somerset Maugham's novel *The Narrow Corner*. In it, the esteemed Dr. Saunders is having a serious discussion with a young chap named Fred Blake. Fred's best friend Erik had committed suicide because of Fred's brief affair with a girl named Louise, and Dr. Saunders tried to console him. Fred wants to know what it all means? Why are we here? Where are we going? What can we do? Dr. Saunders, not giving him an answer, told him people have forever asked these questions.

Eventually, Fred wants to know what Dr. Saunders believes. Dr. Saunders says, "Do you really want to know? I believe in nothing but myself and my experience. The world consists of me and my thoughts and my feelings; and everything else is mere fancy. Life is a dream in which I create the objects that come before me. Everything knowable, every object of experience, is an idea in my mind, and without my mind it does not exist. There is no possibility and no necessity to postulate anything outside myself. Dream and reality are one. Life is a connected and consistent dream, and when I cease to dream, the world, with its beauty, is pain and sorrow, its unimaginable variety, will cease to be."

"But that's quite incredible," cried Fred.

"That is no reason for me to hesitate to believe it," smiled the doctor.

After some more haggling, Fred said to the doctor, "You've lost heart, hope, faith, and awe. What in God's name have you got left?"

"Resignation."

The young man jumped to his feet. "Resignation? That's the refuge of the beaten. Keep your resignation. I don't want it. I'm not willing to accept evil and ugliness and injustice. I'm not willing to stand by while the good are punished and the wicked go scot-free. If life means that virtue is trampled on and honesty is mocked and beauty is fouled, then to hell with life."

"My dear boy, you must take life as you find it," said the doctor.

Resignation is accepting people and things as they are without trying to change them! Recently, I attended a meeting of colleagues. We were asked to submit our agenda items before the meeting, and five minutes prior to closure, the chair remembered that I had some items and asked me if I wanted to speak to them. I declined, because there wasn't enough time left. So, the chair closed the meeting.

What came to my mind was the philosophy of Dr. Saunders in Maugham's novel: Resignation! I actually felt good when I thought about it. Resignation made me deal with the chair's oversight!

When we are young, as Fred was in Maugham's novel, the very notion of resignation is abhorrent, but as we get older and the inevitability of most situations becomes more obvious to us, resignation becomes more and more acceptable as a practical philosophy. This idea is wonderfully expressed by the timeless wisdom of the ancient Serenity Prayer:

God, grant me the serenity to accept the things I cannot change,

The courage to change the things I can,

And the wisdom to know the difference.

Each line represents an important step in our advancement.

In some respects, resignation relates to fatalism, which generally refers to any of the following ideas:

The view that we are powerless to do anything other than what we actually do. Included in this is that humans have no power to influence the future, or indeed, their own actions – very similar to predeterminism; or an attitude of resignation in the face of some future event, which is thought to be inevitable (Friedrich Nietzsche named this idea "Turkish fatalism" in his book *The Wanderer and His Shadow*); or, that acceptance is appropriate, rather than the resistance against inevitability – very similar to defeatism – some take it to mean determinism.

Nevertheless, however well-intentioned the philosophy of resignation may be, one has to be careful that it doesn't lead to apathy!

Generally speaking, many people dislike resignation. The idea doesn't appeal to them because it suggests surrender.

Furthermore, because of its insouciance, the philosophy of resignation may also go through a phase of imagined reality before it ever reaches reality.

Empathy vs Sympathy

According to the dictionary, empathy is the ability to experience the feelings of another person. It goes beyond sympathy, which is caring and understanding for the suffering of others. Both words are used similarly and often interchangeably (incorrectly so) but differ subtly in their emotional meaning.

For example, I sympathize with the British Prime Minister Theresa May regarding her Brexit dilemma, and I sympathize with German Chancellor Angela Merkel regarding her refugee problems, but I cannot offer these two world leaders empathy, because I have never been in this position personally. Empathy they can only expect from each other. So, in October 2018, I wrote Theresa May a letter. I told her that I am a German-born naturalized Canadian citizen, and although I believe Brexit is a mistake because the British people would be better off being part of the European Union, I can sympathize with her position, but that she would be well advised to ask Angela Merkel for help.

I had recommended Angela Merkel because Merkel is also a woman in a world-leader position, and because Merkel has similar problems with her own party, and because Merkel can not only sympathize with May, but she can also empathize with her. I did not get a reply from Theresa May, but I noted that she contacted Angela Merkel several times to get Merkel's help.

As far as empathy on my part is concerned, I can offer this to business managers who are in trouble, because I was a business manager for many years and I have also been in trouble as a business manager. One time, I had lunch with one of my nephews who is managing a construction business. He told me of some of the trouble he was having in his business, and I listened patiently and with empathy, because I could easily put myself in his position. When we finished our lunch, he asked me if I would mind looking at his financial statements, because he was having particular trouble producing a profit for his company. I agreed to have a look at his financial statements, because having empathy with someone also includes offering useful help to that person.

When I had a look at his balance sheet, I saw immediately where he had made his mistake. His assets were mostly non-liquid. We had another lunch together, and I asked him why he insisted on owning land, buildings, heavy equipment, and an unusually large inventory. Ownership of non-liquid assets is attractive to some business managers, but it can be detrimental in the construction business. He said his father, whose business he had taken over, loved owning things. I advised him to sell most of his non-liquid assets and lease what he needs for the business. He took my advice, and after a year he was smiling again. His business was starting to make a profit. Had I not been in a position of empathy to give him advice, any sympathy from me would only have made me feel sorry for him going bankrupt. Empathy helps to imagine the reality and to bring it to a reality.

Of course, one can only offer empathy when one can put oneself in another's position. When one visits friends or relatives lying on their death beds, one can only offer sympathy. Empathy can also be offered to people on their weddings, birthday parties, and travel experiences, which could all be one's own experiences.

Is empathy or sympathy always present in the company of others? No – not always! It is not surprising when someone in the company of his or her peers, who expound their individual miseries with each other, shows no interest, even though he or she could easily empathize with them, or at least sympathize with them. But when his or her feelings of empathy or sympathy are completely turned off, and he or she displays only contempt, the condition is known as apathy. With apathy, there is not even an imagined reality present anymore. The feeling described in the chapter *Resignation* is a form of apathy.

Sometimes movies are made that bring out extraordinary human qualities. If ever a movie was made that brings out empathy, sympathy, compassion, as well as true love and justice, it is *Judgment in Berlin*, with Martin Sheen. The movie dealt with a trial of a couple East Germans accused of highjacking a Polish airplane. Martin Sheen acts as an American judge during the trial, and against the American government's wishes, he insists on jury trial and gets it. Of course, all the jurors are Berliners, and can empathize with the accused, but even the judge and the lawyers and investigators, most of whom are not Berliners, can sympathize with the accused. It is remarkable how well this movie managed to bring out all the various conflicting feelings. Highjacking an airplane is, after all, a terrorists' act, and to empathize with terrorists is nothing short of remarkable.

Compassion goes along with empathy and sympathy. It is not the same as empathy or sympathy, though the concepts are related. People who are kind, caring, and willing to help others, show compassion. A caring nurse is compassionate.

Reasonable Doubt

Criminal cases must be proven beyond a reasonable doubt. If evidence presented by the prosecution leaves a jury with reasonable doubt as to the guilt of the accused, then it must find the accused not guilty. However, sometimes an imagined reality enters into the picture. This happened in a movie called *12 Angry Men*.

In this movie, twelve men on a jury must deliberate on the prosecution's evidence whether or not a teenage boy killed his father. When the jury took an initial vote, eleven men voted "guilty" and one man, juror #8, voted "not guilty." The eleven who voted "guilty" tried to convince juror #8 of their belief, but juror #8 wouldn't budge, and they took another vote. At the second vote, juror #9 also voted "not guilty" and then the jurors started deliberating on the individual evidence that had been presented by the prosecutor.

The boy had claimed he was at a theater watching a movie when the killing took place, but he couldn't remember the name of the movie. Most jurors felt the boy was lying about his alibi. However, the boy could have been telling the truth, which moved this evidence into the area of reasonable doubt as far as the boy's guilt was concerned.

The prosecutor also presented an exceptional knife as the murder weapon, which was rarely available he claimed. The boy had owned such a knife but claimed he had lost it through a hole in his pocket. Juror #8 had gone into the boy's neighborhood and bought a similar knife, thus he proved to the other jurors that a knife like the one used for the killing was not as rare as the prosecutor had claimed, and since the boy could have lost his knife, it also moved this evidence into the area of reasonable doubt as far as the boy's guilt was concerned.

The prosecutor had also presented evidence of an old man who lived in the same apartment building and claimed he had heard shouting and a thump in the boy's apartment and, after it took him fifteen seconds to walk to his stairway door, he saw the boy running away. However, just before and at the time of the killing, an el-train was roaring by their apartments.

Juror #8 had doubts that the old man could have reached the stairway door in fifteen seconds, and proceeded to measure and pace the distance from the old man's bed to the stairway door, which juror #2 timed at forty seconds. This threw doubt on the old man's testimony. In addition, the old man did not see the boy's face; therefore, he could not positively identify him as the boy from the apartment above. Again, it also moved this evidence into the area of reasonable doubt as far as the boy's guilt was concerned.

The boy was also heard shouting "I'll kill you" after his father slapped him. Juror #3 said that anybody who makes such a threat really means it. So, after more discussion, and after juror #3 said he would like to pull the switch to execute the boy, juror #8 provoked juror #3 with some mean accusations, and juror #3 rushed at juror #8 and shouted "I'll kill him; I'll kill him," and two other jurors had to restrain juror #3 from attacking juror #8. Juror #8 just looked at juror #3 and said calmly, "You don't really want to kill me, do you?" Thus, juror #8 made the point that yelling "I'll kill you" is not enough evidence that the boy carried out his threat. More and more jurors voted "not guilty" at ongoing votes, but juror #3 was still adamant that Juror #8 had just "twisted" the evidence to get "not guilty" votes.

A woman who lived in an apartment across the street claimed she saw through an open window the boy killing his father. She was sixty feet away, and the el-train was just roaring by. The prosecutor claimed that a person can see through the windows of a moving el-train when the el-train is nearly empty.

This evidence had many jurors wondering, including juror #8, and they were silent for a while. Then, juror #4 took off his glasses and rubbed the impressions from the glasses on his nose, while suggesting they set a time limit for their discussions. Juror #9 interrupted juror #4 and asked him why he rubbed his nose. Juror #4 told him because it bothered him a little. "Is it because of the glasses' impressions on your nose?" juror #9 asked. "It is," said juror #4, and juror #9 told him he saw those same impressions on the nose of the woman who testified that she saw the boy kill his father. Other jurors chimed in that they saw those impressions on her as well, but juror #3 said they could have been caused by sunglasses which she wore outside and took off inside the court room. Juror #8 asked Juror #4 if the impressions could have been caused by anything but glasses. "No." Juror #8 asked, "Do you wear glasses when you go to sleep?" "No." Juror #4 now had a reasonable doubt and voted "not guilty," that left juror #3 as the only holdout, who finally broke down and said, "Not guilty."

The marks on the woman's nose were not enough to doubt her testimony. The jurors, and the defense lawyer, should have had her eye sight checked. Failing that, the vote should have been "guilty."

This is a typical example of imagined reality.

Business Acumen

Whether just buying or selling stocks in companies, or buying or selling an entire company, or even just running a company, the action often involves an imagined reality. Many investors in company stocks are amateurs. They like the bank they are dealing with, or the company that sells them their favorite coffee, or the company that produces their favorite car model, and they see many other customers who also like their companies, so, they decide to buy some stocks in these companies.

More skilled investors go into further detail before buying or selling stocks in companies. They might look at a company's earnings per share, at a company's book value and debt, its dividend policy, its cash flow, and its management record. Professional investors might even calculate a company's intrinsic stock value. Investment managers who calculate intrinsic values of company stocks are usually known as value investors, who seek stocks they believe the market has undervalued to the companies' intrinsic values. Then, when the market returns the stock prices to their intrinsic values, the investor sells them and seeks other value opportunities. Strictly speaking, this is timing the market to make a profit.

Timing the market is frowned upon by more serious investors, because it can be very risky. When I was still a novice investor, I noticed a chemical company's stock go up and down in the market, although the market itself was fairly stable. After watching several ups and downs of this stock price, I decided to buy it at the low cycle and then sold it at the high cycle. Doing this for a year doubled my initial investment, and I thought I had really caught onto a magic way of making money. Then, one day, the stock did not return to its high cycle but kept on dropping and dropping until the company went belly up, and I lost not only my gains but also my first investment. Obviously, a more careful assessment of the company would have been smarter.

Some professional investors prefer growth stocks over value stocks. They assess companies based on the opportunity to grow their businesses, either by selling more of their products, or by creating new products that are in demand. These investors might buy a company's stock even when the market has already anticipated an amount of growth, believing the amount of growth is still undervalued by the market. This is also an imagined reality, because the growth can't last forever, and the company's stock price will eventually adjust to normal values.

Passive investors invest with a long-term horizon in mind. Rather than timing markets, these investors will create portfolios that track the markets. However, these investors will also be subject to the volatility of the markets, which is a risk few investors can take.

Investors who wish to ignore the volatility of the markets but still earn a decent profit every year usually create portfolios with high dividend-paying stocks. There is something to be said in favor of this type of stock investing. Companies that pay high dividends usually watch their expenses more. CEO's do not get outrageous salaries, and so on. However, occasionally the companies' products are out of favor, and reduced sales can also reduce profits, and with reduced profits these companies might have to reduce their dividends as well. When that happens, the market will punish these companies' stocks. Although a well-diversified, high-dividend investment portfolio can usually weather an occasional company's dividend reduction, and the investor, with his or her steady dividend income, can afford to ignore market volatility, since stocks do not need to be sold to provide the income.

Business acumen is most evident in the construction business. The construction business is particularly subject to various risks that have to be estimated before a bid for a construction project can be submitted and, if these risks are underestimated, they can easily result in business failures. By their very nature, these risk estimates are usually prone to imagined realities.

The construction company usually examines a set of drawings and specifications to determine its interest in the project. Then, to prepare a bid for the project, the company estimates the materials and the labor required, adds the rental cost of tools and equipment for the construction, adds various overheads, and last adds a profit. The profit must not only satisfy its investors but must also cover the construction risks involved. Construction risks involve poor drawing designs, poor weather conditions, underground obstructions, ground contaminations, labor dispute slowdowns, and currency exchange if construction occurs in another country. Then, the construction company assesses the occurrence probability of each risk, and adds an amount to its regular profit markup in case the risk should materialize. These risk calculations are greatly influenced by imagined realities, and different competitors will establish vastly different estimates for them. Even a company that has respectable experience with such risks can lose its bid to less experienced competitors.

Casinos

Talking about business acumen, casinos are top money makers with very little risk involved. In fact, losing money is part of a casino's money-making game, since gamblers count on their luck to win more when casinos lose than lose when casinos win. That illusion is what creates repeat customers for casinos. It is hard to believe that there might be another place than a casino where imagined realities abound except, perhaps, in a church.

Many people like to play the slot machines. There is no skill required. People just imagine that luck will favor them, although they are told that slot machines are programmed to favor the casino. To make slot machines more interesting, casinos have developed quite a few different versions, but all versions are based on the same principle, namely, making sure the casino will be the winner in the end. It is amazing how these machines attract people who believe Lady Luck will favor them. I have watched many times how folks will play their last coins at the Reno or Las Vegas airports in the hope to have some last-minute luck. But the machines end up the winners.

Roulette is another mindless game, similar to slot machines. Favoring the roulette table, people will bet on the favorite number or numbers. People's imagined reality is that these favorite numbers of theirs will bring them more luck in the end than playing other numbers, and, thus, they can win more often and beat the casino. However, they must eventually admit that the roulette tables favor the casinos.

Blackjack is a favorite card game that takes a bit of skill to play. Math wizards have even developed playing methods, which, they believe, will eventually make them steady winners at this game. I have already mentioned this folly in my book *Trials & Errors, Laughs & Terrors*, where Janice, a lady friend of mine, was sold on such a sure winning method, and was shocked that she could not win with it. Here is what I told her: "I think I have found two factors (that put the odds in favor of the casino): The first is a deception: A large number of players believe, naturally, that since the dealer draws on sixteen, the odds must favor him or her to do so. But this is only a ruse, cleverly designed to entice the players to do likewise – draw on sixteen, I mean. The other factor is unfair play: In every tie situation except one, no money changes hands. The exception is a bust. The player who goes bust loses his or her bet, even though the dealer himself may go bust later." However, Janice was still convinced that her winning method would eventually prevail. I like watching people play blackjack, because of their intense facial expressions. Baccarat and poker are also interesting card games to watch in casinos. Craps is a dice game in which the players bet on the outcome of the roll, or a series of rolls, of a pair of dice. I watched craps a few times but have never been too interested in it. It seemed to me too much of a chance game.

When I was in my early twenties, visiting Las Vegas, I let my mental math genius convince me of a fallacy that makes casinos rich. I bet a dollar at a wheel of fortune. The number of dollars on this wheel gave me about a 48% chance of winning. I lost the dollar. Then, to get my dollar back, I bet two dollars on the dollar, and I lost two dollars, and to get my three dollars back, I bet four dollars on the dollar. Then, I made the same mistake as many other fools, and let my logic tell me that the more often the dollar did not win the higher were the odds that it would come up next. Convinced of my logic, I bet eight dollars to get my first dollar back, and I lost again! This four-time loss, instead of discouraging me to bet more, fortified my conviction that surely the wheel must next stop on a dollar. So, I bet sixteen dollars to get my first lost dollar back, and lost again. Did I stop? Not a chance! I bet thirty-two dollars to get my first dollar back, and lost again! Now I knew the next spin of the wheel would finally have to stop on a dollar, and I promptly bet sixty-four dollars, and, guess what? I lost again! So, in for a dollar, in for a pound, as the saying goes, and I bet one hundred and twenty-eight dollars to get my first dollar back! Would you believe that I lost again! Yes, I did! Next came the big decision: do I place another bet on the dollar to get my first lost dollar back or do I quit now? However, the wheel spinner, noticing my hesitation, called a supervisor, because the casino's limit was a $250 bet. The supervisor looked at me, and just said, "Okay." This confidence in me by the supervisor encouraged me to place another bet of two hundred and fifty-six dollars! Let me digress here: to make the trip, I had borrowed five hundred dollars, because I was as poor as a church mouse, as the saying goes, and this last bet cleaned me out! Had I lost it, I would have had to phone home to get my sisters to wire me some money to return to Canada! Guess what: this stupid fool won his last bet, and all he won with his eighth bet was the first dollar he had tried to win – it took $511.00 of bets to win this one dollar! It is a common fallacy of many gamblers to think the odds must eventually change in their favor! Talk about imagined realities: the casinos love them!

Fail-Safe

According to Merriam Webster's, fail-safe is to incorporate some feature for automatically counteracting the effect of an anticipated possible source of failure, or being or relating to a safeguard that prevents continuing on a bombing mission according to a preconceived plan, or having no chance of failure: infallibly problem-free.

The word "ensure" is a very powerful word, it could also stand for some definitions of "fail-safe," like to "ensure" that a feature is in place to offset the effect of a possible source of failure. For example, a few years back, I designed a spreadsheet type of accounting system with a number of cells showing the figure zero, to ensure that every type of entry mistake would be flagged with a figure other than zero in the cell designed to catch a specific mistake. This was a type of fail-safe feature that worked out very well.

World leaders live in imagined realities and have all kinds of fail-safe hitches. Here are some examples:

US President Donald Trump wants to ensure Mexican illegal immigration is eliminated by building a wall along the US-Mexican border. The US constitution assigns congress the power of the purse, and President Trump was circumventing congress to fund the wall by declaring an emergency. On February 18, 2019, sixteen US states filed a lawsuit to stop Trump's national emergency declaration – fail-safe!

United Kingdom Prime Minister Theresa May wants to ensure the UK's economic stability after exiting the UK (Brexit) from the European Union – a tough task for her. More people are now in opposition to Brexit than initially supported it in a referendum. In all probability, if another referendum were being held, Brexiters would lose, because the downsides are now more evident to the people than they had been in 2016.

German Chancellor Angela Merkel wanted to ensure foreign immigration by allowing Middle Eastern refugees into Germany *en masse*. This policy backfired on her when the German population strenuously objected, and she lost too many seats in the following election. Even with fewer seats and negotiating a dubious coalition with an opposition party, her popularity waned further, and she announced her retirement for 2021.

French President Emmanuel Macron wants to ensure the success of his reform program for France despite fierce opposition and violence by the Yellow Jackets. Here is what John Lichfield said on politico: "The bulk of the Yellow Jacket movement decries violence — but also, hypocritically, relies on it. They would not have been able to so quickly extract the concessions they have from Macron if the protests had been merely peaceful and disruptive."

The Spanish new socialist Prime Minister Pedro Sánchez wants to ensure his 2019 budget plan is approved, after the Spanish parliament had rejected it, by calling a snap election to take place in April or May 2019. Thus, he expects the people rather than parliament to approve his budget plans.

The Italian new Prime Minister Giuseppe Conte wants to ensure holding the unusual alliance of the Five Star Movement-League coalition together. Giuseppe Conte is a very religious man, separated from his wife, and may have to serve at the command of the leaders of the two groups forming the new government. Left-wing newspaper La Repubblica marked him as "a prime minister who will not count."

When Greece's Prime Minister Alexis Tsipras ensured a deal on June 12, 2018, with Macedonian Prime Minister Zoran Zaev, to call the ex-Yugoslav republic the Republic of North Macedonia, both Mr. Tsipras and Mr. Zaev were accused in their home countries of national capitulation. The issue had triggered mass protests both in Skopje and Athens. Demonstrations began peacefully attracting more than 200,000 Greeks filling major roads and stopping public transport across Athens. But minutes later, as thousands of protesters continued pouring into Athens, riot police fired tear gas on protesters who tried to break through a security cordon and storm the front gates of the parliament. Obviously, a fail-safe provision was not ensured by Alexis Tsipras!

In a movie called *Fail-Safe* we are shown what can go wrong when there is a fail-safe failure. An error causes an American bomber group to receive orders to attack Moscow. All American attempts to rescind this order fail because a Soviet procedure jams American radio signals. The American President calls the Soviet Chairman and they discuss the American error sending the bombers to Moscow and the Soviets jamming their radio signals, which prevents them from recalling their bombers. The Soviets stop the jamming, but the bomber commander believes the rescinding order is a Soviet ruse. Both countries try to destroy the bombers but one gets through, destroying Moscow, and to appease the Soviets the American President gives an order to destroy New York. What is interesting to me is that Moscow was the center of government for the Soviets, but the American President did not give the order to destroy Washington, DC, the American center of government.

UFOs

A UFO, or unidentified flying object, was reported in ancient Egypt as far back as 1440 BC. According to the disputed Tulli Papyrus, the scribes of the pharaoh Thutmose III reported that "fiery disks" were encountered floating over the skies. Then, in the Roman Republic in 76 BC, according to Pliny the Elder, a spark fell from a star and grew as it descended until it appeared to be the size of the Moon. It then ascended back up to the heavens and was transformed into a light.

However, UFOs, sometimes referred to as flying saucers, became a big fad after World War II, and right through the 1950s and to the end of the 1960s, although sightings are still reported to this day. Even I got caught up in the fad after I returned from a hunting trip and saw a fast moving blip along the horizon, flying parallel to the ground. I knew it could not have been a comet or a meteor or a shooting star because of its parallel flight to the ground, and I knew it could not have been an airplane because it moved many times faster than an airplane; therefore, at the time, I was sure it could only have been a UFO.

In 1947, businessman Kenneth Arnold claimed to have seen a group of nine high-speed objects near Mount Rainier in Washington while flying his small plane. He estimated the speed of the objects at several thousand miles per hour and said they moved "like saucers skipping on water." In the newspaper report that followed, it was mistakenly stated that the objects were saucer-shaped, hence the term flying saucer.[*] This sighting is considered as the start of the "Modern UFO era".[†]

Just as ordinary folks can emerge themselves in mythology, the myths dealing with the gods, demigods, and legendary heroes of a particular people, so can scientist also emerge themselves in questionable beliefs, such as the existence of UFOs. Both are subjects of imagined realities.

An example of this scientific emergence comes from Wilbert B. Smith. He was born February 17, 1910, in Lethbridge, Alberta, graduated from University of British Columbia in 1933 with a BSc in Electrical Engineering and went on to get his MSc in 1934. After university, he became chief engineer for radio station CJOR in Vancouver. I have already mentioned Wilbert B. Smith in my book *Thoughts in a Maze*, with respect to his book titled *The New Science*

---

[*] See the website: http://www.history.com/topics/history-of-ufos
[†] Wikipedia

(1964), but his real hobby was to prove the existence of UFOs.

Here are some excerpts reported by NOUFORS: "During the summer of 1953, Wilbert Smith obtained approval from the Department of Transport (DOT) to set up some UFO detection equipment at Shirley's Bay, near Ottawa, and by the end of October the installation was complete. At 3:01 in the afternoon of August 8, 1954, the instrumentation at the Shirley's Bay installation registered an unusual disturbance. In Smith's words, "the gravimeter went wild." The evidence they had was the deflection registered on the chart recorder paper.

"It has been claimed by some that Smith turned away from orthodox scientific work to the more metaphysical aspects of what he termed 'the new science'. Such was not the case. He carried on his normal scientific work and at the same time, delved into the science of metaphysics as a possible answer to the UFO mystery, which apparently produced some concrete results in the laboratory.

"In the area of metaphysics, Smith claimed to communicate with 'occupants' of UFOs through a contact who provided him with certain information. One instance pertained to areas of reduced binding in our atmosphere. All matter is held together by forces which are not clearly understood and are known as 'binding forces'. Smith was informed that there are areas of reduced binding and that many air crashes were due to entering such regions, where the planes literally fell apart. He was told that means of detecting such areas were easily available to us and that suitable instruments could be constructed. By building a 'binding meter' according to the principles given to him, he was able to locate regions of reduced binding. He recommended to the government that further investigation be conducted, but because of the unorthodox source of his information, he was unable to obtain official recognition of this work and his letters were added to the 'crank file'.

"Smith died of cancer on December 27, 1962. The respect he commanded was reflected in his being posthumously awarded the Lieutenant-Colonel Keith S. Rogers Memorial Engineering Award for dedicated service in the advancement of the Technical Standards in Canadian Broadcasting. This award, presented by the Canadian General Electric Company, was well deserved. Smith was one of the foremost thinkers of his time – a well-respected ufologist – one of the first of our breed."

Well, as I said, UFOs fall into the category of imagined realities, although they may become realities.

Deities and their Spouses

Whether or not the gods of various religions should have also had spouses might be more of a philosophical issue. Some religions openly name the spouses of their deities; other religions are silent about the issue. Of course the duality principle might come into play. If God is a man, there must have been a woman, and vice versa. It is also possible that when men created most religions, they disregarded the importance of women.

In a discussion with a Christian preacher, I asked him why the Bible did not name God's wife. He answered, "Because God did not have a wife."

I told him to open his Bible to Genesis 6, verses 1 and 2.

He did and read aloud, "And it came to pass, when men began to multiply on the face of the earth, and daughters were born onto them, that the sons of God saw the daughters of men that they were fair; and they took them wives of all which they chose."

I said, "So, if God had sons, He must have had a wife! Otherwise, His sons would have been illegitimate! Why did the Bible not name His wife?"

The preacher just looked at me and excused himself because he had a sermon to prepare.

Well, I thought my question was reasonable. Furthermore, if God had sons, it is also justified to assume that God had daughters as well, but the Bible does not mention them, presumably because the daughters were not attracted to human males.

Of course we have Mary, who was a 1st-century BC Galilean Jewish woman of Nazareth, and the mother of Jesus, according to the New Testament and the Quran, and since Jesus was the son of God, Mary can be considered God's wife.

*

Other religions are more open with the names of the spouses of their deities.[*]

Hinduism is the dominant and native/original religion of the Indian subcontinent. It comprises four main traditions: Vaishnavism, Brahmanism, Shaktism, and Saivism, whose followers consider Vishnu, Brahma, Shakti (Devi), and Shiva to be the Supreme deity respectively. The Hindu trinity consists of Brahma the Creator, Vishnu the Preserver, and Shiva the Destroyer. Their feminine counterparts are Saraswati, the wife of Brahma, Lakshmi, the wife of Vishnu, and Parvati, the wife of Shiva.

Buddhism is one of China's main religions.

---

[*] Most of the information comes from Google on the Internet.

Yaśodharā Yaśodharā (Pali: Yasodharā) was the former wife of Gautama Buddha – before he left his home to become a śramaṇa – the mother of Rāhula, and the sister of Devadatta. She later became a bhikkhunī and is considered an arahatā.

To the ancient Greeks, Zeus was the deity who ruled over the sky and weather, and Poseidon was god of the sea. Apollo is the son of Zeus and Leto, and has a twin sister, the chaste huntress Artemis. Zeus has many romantic interests, but he has three wives. The first wife is Metis, who helped him defeat his father Cronus. Metis is the mother of Athena, the goddess of wisdom. Next, Zeus marries Themis, with whom he has six daughters, making him the father of the seasons as well as the Fates. Finally, Zeus marries his sister Hera, who joins him in ruling Mt. Olympus. Leto was one of the Titanides (female Titans), a bride of Zeus, and the mother of the twin gods Apollo and Artemis.

The most important gods to the Romans were the Greek gods from Mount Olympus. The Greek gods were given Roman names, for example, Zeus became Jupiter. Jupiter, Neptune, and Pluto were the three sons of Saturn. Soldiers believed that Mars decided who won, who lost, and who died in battle.

Some sources claim that Al-Lat was the wife of Allah. However, according to Islamic sources, the tribe of Banu Thaqif in Ta'if especially holds reverence to her, but in Islamic tradition, her worship ended when her temple in Ta'if was demolished on the orders of Muhammad.

It is interesting that India and its neighboring countries, like Nepal and Tibet, more readily accept spousal deities than other countries do. Furthermore, wherever powerful deities were invented by males, female deities seem to be secondary, if they exist at all. This practice not only led to male-dominated religions but also to male-dominated societies. Even in the present day, females in these societies must still fight for their equal rights. This is indeed a sad reality! To my personal imagined reality, female deities should be venerated as the truly powerful deities, because our very continuance of the species may be more dependent on females.[*]

---

[*] See the chapter *The End is Near* in my book called *Us Ordinary Folk*.

Feminism

I'm a firm believer in the tremendous ability of women. Men are okay too, as far as it goes, but what I don't like about men is that they start wars too easily. I believe it is women's turn to govern the world for a while.

Feminism is the advocacy of women's rights on the basis of the equality of the sexes. And note this carefully: we're not talking about sameness of the sexes, heavens no; we're talking about equal rights between the sexes, which are many thousands of years overdue!

Sure, in the early days, men had to hunt and fish to bring in food, and women had to cook and look after the babies, but that never gave men the right to take women's rights away from them. Muscle strength does not add rights upon men to bully women into submission. In any case, that's what I believe.

In my book *Conclusions Volume II*, I spent an interlude on women in the news and how their rights were being abused by men. I won't repeat them here, but I can mention some examples that still exist today. As per www.usnews.com, Iraq highly discriminates against its women, and violence against women is common, according to U.N.; Iran is one of six member nations that has not ratified the United Nation's Convention on the Elimination of all Forms of Discrimination Against Women, a decades-old treaty that aims to standardize the rights of women across the globe; and India stands to gain the most from increased gender equality, according to a 2015 report from the McKinsey Global Institute.

As per www.cnn.com, only six countries currently give women and men equal rights, a major report from the World Bank has found. That's an increase – from zero – compared to a decade ago, when the organization started measuring countries by how effectively they guarantee legal and economic equality between the genders. Belgium, Denmark, France, Latvia, Luxembourg, and Sweden scored full marks of 100 in the bank's "*Women, Business, and the Law 2019*" report.

It is interesting that in a union environment the issue of equal rights is not a problem. Many years ago, when most union memberships consisted mainly of men, unions called themselves brotherhoods. But later, when women joined these unions, they were called sisters and given equal rights with their brothers. If the issue of equal rights between the sexes is not a problem in a union environment, why should it be a problem in the rest of the environment?

When I look at women like Theresa May and Angela Merkel, I have nothing but admiration for them – also, Hillary Clinton. She lost the election in 2016 to become the American president, but I believe America and the world had have been better off if she would have won the election. I still don't understand how an intelligent man like Donald Trump manages to offend all of his and America's allies!

Men get offended and go to war; women get offended and try to find a mutually beneficial solution. Am I in love with women? You bet! But it is a love of admiration. I wish, as a man, that I had some of women's qualities. I consult a lot with women because of their deeper insights than men's.

Theresa May is trying to sell Britain's Brexit idea right now. The idea was conceived by ill-informed people who gave her a referendum to go for it. Today, the people, knowing a lot more of the shortcomings of a Brexit, would probably give her a different referendum, but Theresa May does not want to ask for it, because she thinks it might offend the people. She's probably right, but a man would act differently – to hell with the people, if he thinks they are wrong.

Angela Merkel has a soft heart. She was brought up in a Christian religious home. And when desperate refugees wanted to get into Germany, she readily consented. It turned out that this was a mistake, because her world is still governed mostly by men, who disapproved of her soft-hearted approach, and she offered to resign in 2021. This, I think, is a mistake. To put men in their places in this world, you sometimes have to treat them a little rough, as they don't mind treating you.

And what do I think of Hillary Clinton? Well, she missed her chance to beat the bully, but there are other women candidates who want to take him on in 2020, and I hope they have the stamina to stick with it and beat him. Here are the five prominent women who decided to take on the bully: Sen. Elizabeth Warren (D-MA); Rep. Tulsi Gabbard (D-HI); Sen. Amy Klobichar (D-MN); Sen. Kirsten Gillibrand (D-NY); and Sen. Kamala Harris (D-CA).

This is indeed a sign of progress for feminism. It is also an imagined reality that is slowly evolving into a reality. If my prediction comes true, we are getting much closer to women taking over governments and ruling the world, which will be a blessing for all of us. I think the Bible's penalty for women: "*and thy desire shall be to your husband, and he shall rule over thee*," is slowly coming to an end.

Travel Troubles

I like to travel, because it fulfills my imagined realities, at least I hope so before I start out. When I travel, I usually find interesting restaurants to dine at. I remember the time when two friends of mine and I visited San Diego. It was the lobster season and we were enjoying it thoroughly. Then, on the last day at dinner, I mentioned Scoma's Restaurant in San Francisco, and the excellent sand dabs they were serving. Also, Scoma's is one of the few restaurants that still served abalone. My friends were sold, and we decided to stop over in San Francisco.

We arranged to stay in San Francisco for a day, and Scoma's did not disappoint us. However, when we arrived at the airport the following day, Air Canada flights had been cancelled due to an Air Traffic Controllers' strike in Alberta. So, we arranged for an American airline to take us to Spokane. At the Spokane Airport, we stood in line to rent a car to drive back to Alberta. When we reached the desk, we were told that a woman in front of us had just rented the last car the rental agency had available, and she was also heading for Alberta. So, we ran after her and convinced her to let us ride back with her, offering to drive the car for her. I was surprised when she accepted our offer. She was a good looking woman, in her thirties, and I'm not sure what she saw in us that gave her confidence. We reached Banff at 10:00 pm, and stopped for a long-awaited dinner at an excellent restaurant I knew there. It was after midnight when we finally reached Calgary, where our host lady lived. We thanked her again, and promised to have a lunch together as soon as we made another trip to Calgary.

But however good the restaurants are, their food does not always agree with my constitution.

This brings to mind a restaurant in New Orleans, one of my favorite cities, which I visited in November 1983. New Orleans provides excellent entertainment, and in November the oysters are delicious. Some people like oysters fried, but connoisseurs usually like them raw. In fact, still alive, right from the shell.

I was sitting at the restaurant's bar counter, enjoying a glass of white wine, and watching the bar tender chuck live oysters. Everybody at the counter ordered a dozen oysters, and I decided to join them. The bar tender served a special sauce to go with the oysters, and my first dozen oysters disappeared in a matter of minutes. The bar tender gave me a questioning look, and I gave him a nod. My second dozen oysters disappeared almost as fast as the first dozen, and my stomach told me I've had enough. But as is so often the case when food tastes too good, the warning of one's stomach gets ignored, and when the bar tender gave me another questioning look, I gave him another nod. After finishing the third dozen of oysters, I couldn't remember when my stomach was ever that full.

I survived the meal and the trip, but soon afterwards my prostate started to hurt me. The pain became gradually worse, and I went to see my doctor. He gave me a finger test and declared flatly "prostatitis." He told me that prostatitis is a low-grade infection that is hard to treat and can take several years to heal, if it heals at all. He sent me to a urologist to make sure it's nothing more serious, and the urologist also gave me a finger test and then scheduled me for a cystoscopy. The cystoscopy did not reveal anything more serious than a slightly swollen prostate, and the urologist prescribed some medication to treat the prostatitis. Some of my friends told me that one has to pay for his sins, even before judgment day. Well, I can attest to that statement. It took many years to get rid of the prostatitis, and, I should add, even without more oysters.

One trip that stands out most in my mind is a trip I took to Saudi Arabia. It was a trip two friends of mine and I took at the invitation of a sheik, related to the doctor of the king. Before the trip, my imagined realities included tales of the Arabian Nights, belly dancers, and exotic food. However, the reality I met up with was disappointing to say the least. When we arrived at the airport in Jeddah, we were met by several military policemen pointing AK-47 assault rifles at us. It took us forty-five minutes to get through the Saudi security. Our luggage was checked, but the only warning they gave us was not to take pictures at the airport and at the harbor. We had rooms, more like suites, at the Le Méridien Hotel.

On the second day after our arrival, we met with the sheik, and he instructed his manager to take us to lunches and dinners. I had no idea how many lamb dishes can be created until I arrived in Saudi Arabia. The souk in Jeddah was absolutely amazing: piles of American dollars right up to the ceiling at the money changers; gold jewelry galore; Arabian men sitting in the streets smoking their water pipes; and so on. However, on the way home, the airport turned out to be a nightmare. The Lufthansa Airline told us to report at 6:00 pm for a flight that was scheduled to take off at 2:00 am the next morning, and with all the Saudi and Airline security checks, we almost missed our flight. Moral: Be careful what kind of reality you imagine!

Overconservatism

If one is interested in the effects of overconservatism, one only needs to analyze defined-benefit pension plans. Trustees of these plans, anxious to protect their pension promise, will want some conservatism; their actuary, anxious to justify his or her calculations, will want some conservatism; in addition, the government, anxious to escape criticism, enacts ultraconservative pension laws and regulations. These three conservative approaches can easily lead to overconservatism. For example, if each party allows about 20% to cover his or her conservatism, only 51.2% of a pension fund's assets will be available for pensions; the other 48.8% end up in reserves to cover these three conservatisms.

A huge number of people depend on a pension for their retirement. Many employers provide pensions or assist employees during retirement. The two main types of pension plans are either based on defined contributions or on defined benefits.

A defined contribution plan is based solely on contributions – a type of savings plan to which both the employer and the employee can contribute, and any earnings and/or losses accrue to the employee in whose name the plan is registered.

A defined benefit pension plan also depends on contributions, mostly made by the employer, and the benefit to the employee can be higher than the contributions made for his or her work because of subsidizations. For example, the contributions may adequately provide for a pension if an employee retires at age 65 and dies at age 83, but should the employee retire at an earlier age or die at a later age, the pension is usually subsidized by employees who retire at age 65 or later and/or die at age 83 or earlier. This subsidization can be fairly easily reconciled by an actuary. Some employees benefit, other employees lose. The pension plan comes out even.

A problem arises when pension regulators get involved with defined benefit pension plans. Pension regulators want to protect the pension promises made by employers to employees, and in their enthusiasm to protect, pension regulators often interfere with and criticize the assumptions actuaries make to establish reasonable pensions of defined benefit plans.

For example, an actuary might establish a pension liability by assuming that the pension plan will earn a 7% return per annum on its investments in the long run, but the pension regulator might disagree with this assumption and demand an assumption of

6% per annum should be used, which the pension regulator claims is more realistic. However, this lower assumption will substantially increase the plan's pension liability for the promised pensions, and, thus, disallow pension increases to keep up with cost-of-living increases.

All of the actuaries' assumptions[*] are similarly criticized by pension regulators. Pension regulators are inherently pessimistic about the future. However, it must be said that actuaries, to assure their assumptions do not backfire on them, are already fairly conservative when arriving at their assumptions. Thus, employees and pensioners are hit with a double whammy: once by the actuaries, and then by the pension regulators.

Of course, any money earned over and above an actuary's assumptions doesn't disappear, it is simply available to future pensioners, and, thus, represents another subsidy provided by all the current pensioners to future pensioners. The fact that a country's Constitution[†] and Trustee Act[‡] that provide equal

---

[*] Such as retirement rates, post-retirement mortality rates, termination rates, hours-worked estimates, and so on.

[†] Section 15 of the Canadian Charter of Rights and Freedoms contains guaranteed equality rights. This section states: Every individual is equal before and under the law and has the right to the equal protection and equal benefit of the law without discrimination...

[‡] The Alberta Trustee Act, Section 3(5)(b) the duty to act impartially towards beneficiaries and between different classes of beneficiaries.

treatment to employees and pensioners are being violated does not seem to be of concern to pension regulators, or, for that matter, actuaries. To add insult to injury, pension regulators also want a provision for adverse deviation, just in case the stock market behaves badly. This would further decrease the already decreased 6% per annum annual return assumption to approximately 5%, for a very unreasonable increase in the pension liability.

Evidently, both pension regulators and actuaries act from an imagined reality, which can lower pensions by as much as 50%, at the expense of present pensioners who must cope with a reality that denies them adequate compensation for cost-of-living adjustments.

The principle of equality is one of the most important principles in our times. When pension regulators ignore this principle, it makes us wonder about their sincerity – even though pension regulators are trying their best to protect those whom they betray by ignoring this principle. Both a pension plan's trustees and their actuary must try everything possible to ensure that this equality principle is upheld.

Will the Future be better?

This year (2019) I completed forty-eight years as a trustee. I can tell you with certainty that I enjoyed the first half of my trusteeship more than the second half, even though the first half entailed most of the trust establishment work, and we did not receive any remuneration for the first few years. However, we had time to do all of the trustees' work; we had time for each other; we had time for ourselves; and we had time to enjoy all of it. But in the second half of my trusteeship most of the enjoyment I had experienced in the first half disappeared, and only the drudging work remained.

Now, will the future be better or worse than the past? Based on my experience as a trustee, I'm not sure how to answer this question, although I'm of the opinion that generally speaking the future will always be better than the past.

I asked a group of contractors this question two years ago, and I was surprised that over 70% said the future will be worse. Then, a year later, I requested the same group to mentally imagine themselves to be back in the year 1800 and be asked if the future would be better or worse than the past, not knowing what they know now. I had them puzzled for a while. Then, I projected for them the following list of things that did not yet exist in 1800:

- No useful use of electricity yet
- No electric light bulbs
- No electric motors
- No forced-air furnaces
- No steam-engine train yet
- No buses
- No cars
- No planes
- No radios
- No telephones
- No TVs
- No computers
- No Internet
- No space travel
- No Moon and Mars landings
- Etcetera

Quite obviously to my contractor friends seeing this list, the future was better than the past in 1800, and still is.

When I had asked these contractors the original

question, it had been after discussing the trust fund's investment returns. Our board of trustees had achieved an average yearly return since inception of over nine percent, yet our pension regulators had a problem with our actuary's proposal using a discount assumption that was one-third less than our historic return. In addition to this reduction, the pension regulators also want a provision for adverse deviation, which comes to another seventeen percent reserve. Obviously, the pension regulators' crystal ball not only predicted a future return one-third less than the trustees' historical return, but then needed another seventeen percent assurance in case the market behaved adversely. For the regulators, the future is very much worse than the past – all at the expense of our present pensioners, of course.

The pension regulators are only looking at stock markets for their opinion, but stock markets are mostly driven by the whim of sellers and buyers of securities, less so by the qualities of the companies that make up the market. And, with most companies, the future is normally better than the past.

Many people will think only of themselves when trying to answer this question – I'm growing older; that's not better; I'm more prone to illnesses as I grow older; that's not better; I can't hear and see as well as I used to; that's not better; I can't walk as well as I used to; that's not better; what will happen to me after I die; and so on.

Things that could be better for future generations do not concern these people anymore, unless they could be part of it. Their imagined reality is self-centered rather than community-centered. They may leave a few dollars behind for their inheritors, that's all. Behind them comes the Great Flood, as my mother liked to say.

Appendix

The following excerpts are taken from my book
Exposed to Winds:

*

How many "good" books do we read in vain?
And how many to find a new way?
How many books will provide us a gain?
And how many more lead us astray?

*

Our knowledge is so limited in sphere
That all we comprehend is now and here;
To know eternity's as folly to pretend
As knowing where beginning meets its very end!

*

Nor is the wisdom we may gain of use
If used in ignorance of love each year:
Most things we know just serve us to confuse
The reasons why we live and why we're here.

*

And, strange enough, a happiness ensues:
A happiness that has no further use
Of cultural development of mind,
Or any other intellectual kind.

Great is the purpose that forgets the now
And questions all of future's where and how
Without ulterior motive in the mind:
The ultimate perfection for mankind!

*

When we go astray, when we miss the mark,
We must pay to get back on course;
Sometimes it seems that the price is too high,
But balance demands this with force!

*

You cannot balance poor quality
With an increase in the amount:
It is best to forget about quantity
When you balance this type of account.

*

Only when I look inside me
Do I know I'm on the track;
Do I know to go on safely,
Not desiring to look back.

*

About the Author

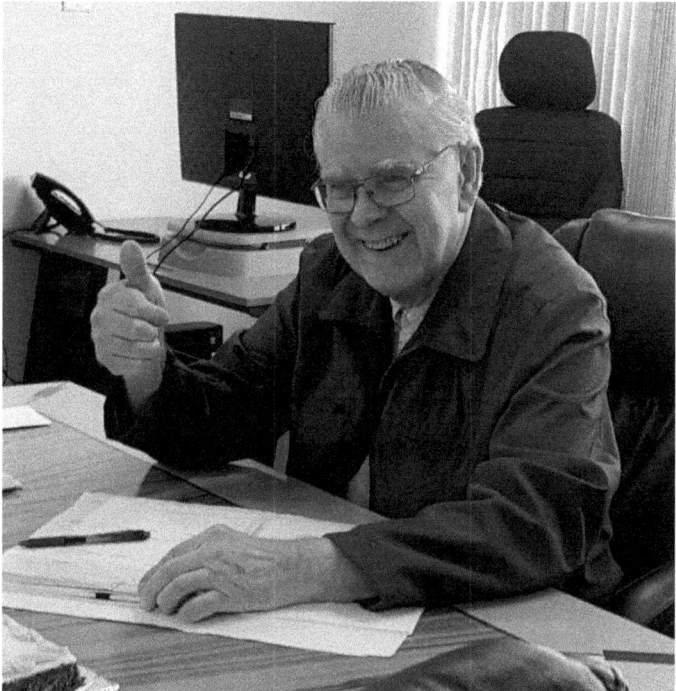

Arthur Thormann was born in Berlin, Germany, in 1934. He came to Canada at age 17 in 1951, and became a naturalized Canadian in 1957. He loves Canadians more than any other people, and thinks Canadians are probably the most democratic people in the world.